Contents

The Promises of the Moment:

What the Manger Means to Me

Epilogue:

Silent Night of the Heart

Preface

*T*here is one word that describes the night He came—ordinary.

The sky was ordinary. An occasional gust stirred the leaves and chilled the air. The stars were diamonds sparkling on black velvet. Fleets of clouds floated in front of the moon.

It was a beautiful night—a night worth peeking out your bedroom window to admire—but not really an unusual one. No reason to expect a surprise. Nothing to keep a person awake. An ordinary night with an ordinary sky.

The sheep were ordinary. Some fat. Some scrawny. Some with barrel bellies. Some with twig legs. Common animals. No fleece made of gold. No history makers. No blue-ribbon winners. They were simply sheep—lumpy, sleeping silhouettes on a hillside.

And the shepherds. Peasants they were. Probably wearing all the clothes they owned. Smelling like sheep and looking just as woolly. They were conscientious, willing to spend the night with their flocks. But you won't find their staffs in a museum nor their writings in a library. No one asked their opinion on social justice or the application of the Torah. They were nameless and simple.

An ordinary night with ordinary sheep and ordinary shepherds. And were it not for a God who loves to hook an "extra" on the front of the ordinary, the night would have gone unnoticed. The sheep would have been forgotten, and the shepherds would have slept the night away.

But God dances amidst the common. And that night he did a waltz.

The black sky exploded with brightness. Trees that had been shadows jumped into clarity. Sheep that had been silent became a chorus of curiosity. One minute the shepherd was dead asleep, the next he was rubbing his eyes and staring into the face of an alien.

The night was ordinary no more.

MAX LUCADO
THE APPLAUSE OF HEAVEN

A G I F T F O R :

. . . .

B y :

. . . .

O come, let us adore Him,

Christ the Lord.

—Latin Carol, 18th century

One Incredible Moment

Celebrating the Majesty of the Manger

From the Writings of

MAX LUCADO

Silent Night! Holy Night!

All is calm, all is bright.

Round yon virgin mother and child!

Holy Infant so tender and mild,

Sleep in heavenly peace, sleep in heavenly peace!

—JOSEPH MOHR, 1818

What child is this, who,

laid to rest

On Mary's lap, is sleeping?…

This, this is Christ the King,

Whom shepherds guard and angels sing:

Haste, haste to bring Him laud,

The Babe, the Son of Mary!

—Traditional English Carol

The Ones Who
Knew Him First

O little town of Bethlehem,

How still we see thee lie!

Above thy deep and dreamless sleep

The silent stars go by.

Yet in thy dark streets shineth

The everlasting Light;

The hopes and fears of all the years

Are met in thee tonight.

PHILLIPS BROOKS, 1867

From One Father to Another

This isn't the way I planned it, God. Not at all. My child being born in a stable? This isn't the way I thought it would be. A cave with sheep and donkeys, hay and straw? My wife giving birth with only the stars to hear her pain?

This isn't at all what I imagined. No, I imagined family. I imagined grandmothers. I imagined neighbors clustered outside the door and friends standing at my side. I imagined the house erupting with the first cry of the infant. Slaps on the back. Loud laughter. Jubilation.

That's how I thought it would be. . . .

But now. . . . Who will celebrate with us? The sheep? The shepherds? The stars?

This doesn't seem right. What kind of husband am I? I provide no midwife to aid my wife. No bed to rest her back. Her pillow is a blanket from my donkey. . . .

Did I miss something? Did I, God?

When you sent the angel and spoke of the son being born—this isn't what I pictured. I envisioned Jerusalem, the temple, the priests, and the people gathered to watch. A pageant perhaps. A parade. . . . I mean, this is the Messiah!

Or, if not born in Jerusalem, how about Nazareth? Wouldn't Nazareth have been better? At least there I have my house and my business. Out here, what do I have? A weary mule, a stack of firewood, and a pot of warm water. This is not the way I wanted it to be! . . . Forgive me for asking but . . . is this how God enters the world? The coming of the angel, I've accepted. The questions people asked about the pregnancy, I can tolerate. The trip to Bethlehem, fine. But why a birth in a stable, God?

Any minute now Mary will give birth. Not to a child, but to the Messiah. Not to an infant, but to God. That's what the angel said. That's what Mary believes. And God, my God, that's what I want to believe. But surely you can understand; it's not easy. It seems so . . . so . . . so . . . bizarre.

I'm unaccustomed to such strangeness, God. I'm a carpenter. I make things fit. I square off the edges. I follow the plumb line. I measure twice before I cut

once. Surprises are not the friend of a builder. I like to know the plan. I like to see the plan before I begin.

But this time I'm not the builder, am I? This time I'm a tool. A hammer in your grip. A chisel in your hands. This project is yours, not mine.

I guess it's foolish of me to question you. Forgive my struggling. Trust doesn't come easy to me, God. But you never said it would be easy, did you? . . .

One final thing, Father. The angel you sent? Any chance you could send another? If not an angel, maybe a person? I don't know anyone around here and some company would be nice. Maybe the innkeeper or a traveler? Even a shepherd would do.

HE STILL MOVES STONES

The angel said,

"Joseph, descendant of David,

don't be afraid to take Mary as your wife,

because the baby in her is from the Holy Spirit.

She will give birth to a son,

and you will name him Jesus,

because he will save

his people from their sins."

MATTHEW 1:20–21

Mary's Prayer

God. O infant-God. Heaven's fairest child. Conceived by the union of divine grace with our disgrace. Sleep well.

Sleep well. Bask in the coolness of this night bright with diamonds. Sleep well, for the heat of anger simmers nearby. Enjoy the silence of the crib, for the noise of confusion rumbles in your future. Savor the sweet safety of my arms, for a day is soon coming when I cannot protect you.

Rest well, tiny hands. For though you belong to a king, you will touch no satin, own no gold. You will grasp no pen, guide no brush. No, your tiny hands are reserved for works more precious:

to touch a leper's open wound,

to wipe a widow's weary tear,

to claw the ground of Gethsemane.

Your hands, so tiny, so tender, so white—clutched tonight in an infant's fist. They aren't destined to hold a scepter nor wave from a palace balcony. They are reserved instead for a Roman spike that will staple them to a Roman cross.

Sleep deeply, tiny eyes. Sleep while you can. For soon the blurriness will clear and you will see the mess we have made of your world.

You will see our nakedness, for we cannot hide.

You will see our selfishness, for we cannot give.

You will see our pain, for we cannot heal.

O eyes that will see hell's darkest pit and witness her ugly prince . . . sleep, please sleep; sleep while you can.

Lay still, tiny mouth. Lay still mouth from which eternity will speak.

Tiny tongue that will soon summon the dead,

that will define grace,

that will silence our foolishness.

Rosebud lips—upon which ride a starborn kiss of forgiveness to those who believe you, and of death to those who deny you—lay still.

And tiny feet cupped in the palm of my hand, rest. For many difficult steps lie ahead for you. . . .

Do you feel the cold sea water upon which you will walk?

Do you wrench at the invasion of the nail you will bear?

Do you fear the steep descent down the spiral staircase into Satan's domain?

Rest, tiny feet. Rest today so that tomorrow you might walk with power. Rest. For millions will follow in your steps.

And little heart . . . holy heart . . . pumping the blood of life through the universe: How many times will we break you?

You'll be torn by the thorns of our accusations.

You'll be ravaged by the cancer of our sin.

You'll be crushed under the weight of your own sorrow.

And you'll be pierced by the spear of our rejection.

Yet in that piercing, in that ultimate ripping of muscle and membrane, in that final rush of blood and water, you will find rest. Your hands will be freed, your eyes will see justice, your lips will smile, and your feet will carry you home.

And there you'll rest again—this time in the embrace of your Father.

GOD CAME NEAR

My soul praises the Lord;
my heart rejoices in God my Savior,
because he has shown his concern
for his humble servant girl.
From now on,
all people will say that I am blessed,
because the Powerful One has done
great things for me.

LUKE 1:46–49

The Meek Were Kneeling

lessed are the meek," Jesus explained. Blessed are the available. Blessed are the conduits, the tunnels, the tools. . . .

That's why the announcement went first to the shepherds. They didn't ask God if he was sure he knew what he was doing. Had the angel gone to theologians, they would have first consulted their commentaries. Had he gone to the elite, they would have looked around to see if anyone was watching. Had he gone to the successful, they would have first looked at their calendars.

So he went to the shepherds. Men who didn't have a reputation to protect or an ax to grind or a ladder to climb. Men who didn't know enough to tell God that angels don't sing to sheep and that messiahs aren't found wrapped in rags and sleeping in a feed trough. . . .

A small cathedral outside Bethlehem marks the supposed birthplace of Jesus.

While shepherds
watch'd their flocks by night
All seated on the ground,
The angel of the Lord came down,
And glory shone around.
"Fear not," said he, for mighty dread
had seized their troubled mind;
"Glad tiding of great joy I bring
to you and all mankind."

—NAHUM TATE, 1700

Behind a high altar in the church is a cave, a little cavern lit by silver lamps.

You can enter the main edifice and admire the ancient church. You can also enter the quiet cave where a star embedded in the floor recognizes the birth of the King. There is one stipulation, however. You have to stoop. The door is so low you can't go in standing up.

The same is true of the Christ. You can see the world standing tall, but to witness the Savior, you have to get down on your knees.

So . . .

while the theologians were sleeping

and the elite were dreaming

and the successful were snoring,

the meek were kneeling.

They were kneeling before the One only the meek will see. They were kneeling in front of Jesus.

THE APPLAUSE OF HEAVEN

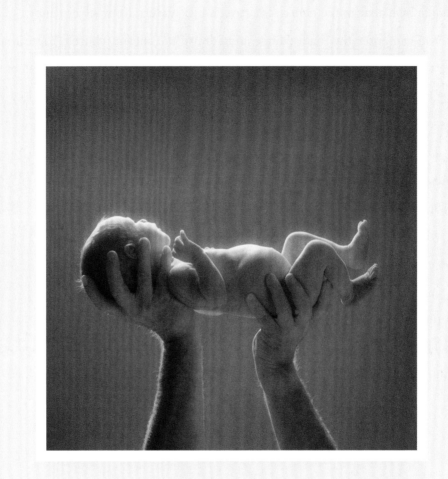

Simeon: Wide-eyed and Watching

"Now in Jerusalem there was a man named Simeon. He was an upright and devout man; he *looked forward* to Israel's comforting and the Holy Spirit rested on him" (Luke 2:25 tjb, emphasis mine).

Let's imagine a white-headed, wizened fellow working his way down the streets of Jerusalem. People in the market call his name and he waves but doesn't stop. Neighbors greet him and he returns the greeting but doesn't pause. Friends chat on the corner and he smiles but doesn't stop. He has a place to be and he hasn't time to lose.

Simeon: the man who knew how to wait for the arrival of Christ. The way he waited for the first coming is a model for how we should wait for the Second Coming.

Simeon's one incredible moment occurs eight days after the birth of Jesus.

When Mary and Joseph
brought the baby Jesus to the Temple
to do what the law said they must do,
Simeon took the baby in his arms
and thanked God:
"Now, Lord, you can let me, your servant,
die in peace as you said.
With my own eyes
I have seen your salvation...."

LUKE 2:27-30

Joseph and Mary have brought their son to the temple. It's the day of a sacrifice, the day of circumcision, the day of dedication. But for Simeon, it's the day of celebration.

Verse 27 contains this curious statement: "Prompted by the Spirit he came to the Temple." Simeon apparently had no plans to go to the temple. God, however, thought otherwise. We don't know how the prompting came—a call from a neighbor, an invitation from his wife, a nudging within the heart—we don't know. But somehow Simeon knew to clear his calendar and put away his golf clubs. "I think I will go to church," he announced.

On this side of the event, we understand the prompting. Whether Simeon understood or not, we don't know. We do know, however, that this wasn't the first time God tapped him on the shoulder. At least one other time in his life, he had received a message from God.

"The Holy Spirit had revealed to him that he would not die until he had seen him—God's anointed King" (v. 26 TLB).

You've got to wonder what a message like that would do to a person. What does it do to you if you know you will someday see God? We know what it did to Simeon.

He was "constantly expecting the Messiah" (v. 25 TLB).

He was "living in expectation of the salvation of Israel" (v. 25 PHILLIPS).

He "watched and waited for the restoration of Israel" (v. 25 NEB).

Simeon is a man on tiptoe, wide-eyed and watching for the one who will come to save Israel. . . .

The Greek language, rich as it is with terms, has a stable full of verbs that mean "to look." One means to "look up," another "look away;" one is used to "look upon" and another "looking in." To "look at something intently" requires one word and to "look over someone carefully" mandates another.

Of all the forms of *look,* the one that best captures what it means to "look for the coming" is the term used to describe the action of Simeon: *prosdechomai.* *Dechomai* meaning "to wait." *Pros* meaning "forward." Combine them and you have the graphic picture of one "waiting forwardly." The grammar is poor, but the image is great. Simeon was waiting; not demanding, not hurrying, he was waiting.

But he was waiting with anticipation. Calmly expectant. Eyes open. Arms extended. Searching the crowd for the right face, and hoping the face appears today. . . .

In the end, the prayer of Simeon was answered. "Simeon took the baby in his arms and thanked God; 'Now, Lord, you can let me, your servant, die in peace, as you said'" (LUKE 2:28–29).

One look into the face of Jesus, and Simeon knew the hope of his life had been fulfilled. One look into the face of our Savior, and we will know the same.

WHEN CHRIST COMES

Following the Star

Suppose you could give a gift to Christ, what would it be? How could you possibly select a gift for the One who not only has everything, but who made everything?

The Wise Men did. They can be an example to us. In addition to the gold, frankincense, and myrrh, they gave the Savior some gifts we can give him today: their hope, their time, and their worship.

The wandering wise men gave Jesus their hope. When everyone else saw a night sky, this small band of men saw the light. The sight of the star sparked a desire in their hearts that sent them packing. They went, seeking Jesus.

When night comes to your world, what do you see? The darkness or the stars? Hopelessness or hopefulness? Sometimes, just as he did so long ago, God uses the darkness to reveal his stars—"The light shines in the darkness" (JOHN 1:5). If your heart has been shadowed by the darkness of loneliness or grief or disappointment, look for the light that only he can give. "I am the light of the world. The person who follows me will never live in darkness but will have the light that gives life" (JOHN 8:12).

Give God your hope for Christmas.

While you're giving, give God your time. The wise men did. Before they gave God their presents, they gave their *presence*. It's likely that these men traveled as long as two years before locating the prince of heaven. Before that one incredible moment when they knelt before Jesus, the wise men spent many moments, months, perhaps years searching, in anticipation of that meeting. Just as the wise men devoted themselves to seeking the Savior, so can you: "You will seek him and find him when you seek him with all of your heart" (DEUT. 4:29).

And when they did find him, the wise men gave Jesus another gift: their worship. It's probable that these were men of wealth. (How else could they embark on an extended journey and still have gifts to give at its end?) It's likely these men had influence. (How else could they have commanded an audience with Herod?) They must have had intellect. (How else could they have navigated across thousands of miles of terrain following a star?)

Men of wealth, influence, and intellect: what did they do when they saw

Come to Bethlehem and see

Him whose birth the angels sing;

Come adore, on bended knee,

Christ, the Lord, the newborn King.

Gloria, in excelsius Deo.

—Traditional French Carol

Jesus? ". . . They fell down and *worshiped* him" (MATT. 2:11).

Worship. It's a gift that extends to the giver as well. Through worship, we come to see God more clearly. God invites us, through worship, to see his face so he can change ours. "We all show the Lord's glory, and we are being changed to be like him. This change in us brings ever greater glory, which comes from the Lord, who is the Spirit" (2 COR. 3:18).

He loves to change the faces of his children. By his fingers, wrinkles of worry are rubbed away. Shadows of shame and doubt become portraits of grace and trust. He relaxes clenched jaws and smoothes furrowed brows. . . .

In worship, we simply stand before God with a prepared and willing heart and let God do his work. And he does. He wipes away the tears. He mops away the perspiration. He softens our furrowed brows. He touches our cheeks. He changes our faces as we worship.

The wise men sought the child of God, just as God seeks his children. "The Father is actively seeking such people to worship him" (JOHN 4:23).

The gifts of hope, time, and worship. Three gifts the wise still give.

JUST LIKE JESUS

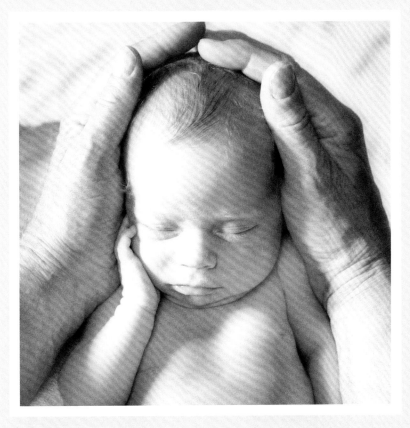

THE PASSION OF THE MOMENT

Thoughts
on God's Love

God's love had no strings,

no expectations,

no hidden agendas, no secrets.

His love for us was, and is,

up front and clear.

Love's Remarkable Plan

Seated at the great desk, the Author opens the large book. It has no words. It has no words because no words exist. No words exist because no words are needed. There are no ears to hear them, no eyes to read them. The Author is alone.

And so he takes the great pen and begins to write. Like an artist gathers his colors and a woodcarver his tools, the Author assembles his words.

There are three. Three single words. Out of these three will pour a million thoughts. But on these three words, the story will suspend.

He takes his quill and spells the first. *T-i-m-e*.

Time did not exist until he wrote it. He, himself, is timeless, but his story would be encased in time. The story would have a first rising of the sun, a first

Come, thou long-expected Jesus,
Born to set thy people free;
From our fears and sins release us,
Let us find our rest in thee.

—CHARLES WESLEY, 1744

shifting of the sand. A beginning . . . and an end. A final chapter. He knows it before he writes it.

Time. A footspan on eternity's trail.

Slowly, tenderly, the Author writes the second word. A name. *A-d-a-m*.

As he writes, he sees him, the first Adam. Then he sees all of the others. In a thousand eras in a thousand lands, the Author sees them. Each Adam. Each child. Instantly loved. Permanently loved. To each he assigns a time. To each he appoints a place. No accidents. No coincidences. Just design.

The Author makes a promise to these unborn: *In my image, I will make you. You will be like me. You will laugh. You will create. You will never die. And you will write.*

They must. For each life is a book, not to be read, but rather a story to be written. The Author starts each life story, but each life will write his or her own ending.

What a dangerous liberty. How much safer it would have been to finish the story for each Adam. To script every option. It would have been simpler. It would have been safer. But it would not have been love. Love is only love if chosen.

So the Author decides to give each child a pen. "Write carefully," he whispers.

Lovingly, deliberately, he writes a third word, already feeling the pain. *E-m-m-a-n-u-e-l*.

The greatest mind in the universe imagined time. The truest judge granted Adam a choice. But it was love that gave Emmanuel, God with us.

The Author would enter his own story.

The Word became flesh. He, too, would be born. He, too, would be human. He, too, would have feet and hands. He, too, would have tears and trials.

And most importantly, he, too, would have a choice. Emmanuel would stand at the crossroads of life and death and make a choice.

The Author knows well the weight of that decision. He pauses as he writes the page of his own pain. He could stop. Even the Author has a choice. But how can a Creator not create? How can a Writer not write? And how can Love not love? So he chooses life, though it means death, with hope that his children will do the same.

And so the Author of Life completes the story. He drives the spike in the flesh and rolls the stone over the grave. Knowing the choice he will make, knowing the choice all Adams will make, he pens, "The End," then closes the book and proclaims the beginning.

"Let there be light!"

A Gentle Thunder

To Win Your Love

ere is what we want to know. We want to know how long God's love will endure. . . . Does God really love us forever? Not just on . . . Sunday when our shoes are shined and our hair is fixed. We want to know . . . how does God feel about me when I'm a jerk? Not when I'm peppy and positive and ready to tackle world hunger. Not then. I know how he feels about me then. Even I like me then.

I want to know how he feels about me when I snap at anything that moves, when my thoughts are gutter-level, when my tongue is sharp enough to slice a rock. How does he feel about me then? . . .

Can anything separate us from the love Christ has for us?

God answered our question before we asked it. So we'd see his answer, he lit the sky with a star. So we'd hear it, he filled the night with a choir;

Joy to the world!
the Lord is come:
Let Earth receive her King;
Let every heart prepare Him room,
And heaven and nature sing.

—Isaac Watts

and so we'd believe it, he did what no man had ever dreamed. He became flesh and dwelt among us.

He placed his hand on the shoulder of humanity and said, "You're something special."

In the Grip of Grace

Timeless, Boundless Love

Untethered by time, [God] sees us all. From the backwoods of Virginia to the business district of London; from the Vikings to the astronauts, from the cave-dwellers to the kings, from the hut-builders to the finger-pointers to the rock-stackers, he sees us. Vagabond and ragamuffins all, he saw us before we were born.

And he loves what he sees. Flooded by emotion. Overcome by pride, the Starmaker turns to us, one by one, and says, "You are my child. I love you dearly. I'm aware that someday you'll turn from me and walk away. But I want you to know, I've already provided a way back."

And to prove it, he did something extraordinary.

Stepping from the throne, he removed his robe of light and wrapped himself in skin: pigmented, human skin. The light of the universe entered a dark, wet womb. He whom angels worship nestled himself in the placenta of a peasant, was birthed into a cold night, and then slept on cow's hay.

Mary didn't know whether to give him milk or give him praise, but she gave him both since he was, as near as she could figure, hungry and holy.

Joseph didn't know whether to call him Junior or Father. But in the end he called him Jesus, since that's what the angel had said and since he didn't have the faintest idea what to name a God he could cradle in his arms. . . .

Don't you think . . . their heads tilted and their minds wondered, "What in the world are you doing, God?" Or, better phrased, "God, what are you doing in the world?"

"Can anything make me stop loving you?" God asks. "Watch me speak your language, sleep on your earth, and feel your hurts. Behold the maker of sight and sound as he sneezes, coughs, and blows his nose. You wonder if I understand how you feel? Look into the dancing eyes of the kid in Nazareth: that's God walking to school. Ponder the toddler at Mary's table; that's God spilling his milk.

"You wonder how long my love will last? Find your answer on a splintered cross, on a craggy hill. That's me you see up there, your maker, your God, nail-stabbed and bleeding. Covered in spit and sin-soaked.

"That's your sin I'm feeling. That's your death I'm dying. That's your resurrection I'm living. That's how much I love you."

In the Grip of Grace

A Little Piece of Heaven

How great is God's love? How can the creator of the universe care about the twists and turns of your life's journey? Ponder this thought:

If God is able to place the stars in their sockets and suspend the sky like a curtain, do you think it remotely possible that God is able to guide your life? If your God is mighty enough to ignite the sun, could it be that he is mighty enough to light your path? If he cares enough about the planet Saturn to give it rings or Venus to make it sparkle, is there an outside chance that he cares enough about you to meet your needs? Or, as Jesus says,

Look at the birds in the air. They don't plant or harvest
or store into barns, but your heavenly Father feeds them.
And you know you are worth much more than the

birds. . . .Why do you worry about clothes?

Look at how the lilies in the field grow.

They don't work or make clothes for themselves.

But I tell you that even Solomon with his

riches was not dressed as beautifully as one of these flowers.

God clothes the grass in the field,

which is alive today but tomorrow is thrown into the fire.

So you can even be sure that God will clothe you.

Don't have so little faith!

(MATT. 6:25–30)

Why did he do it? Did he have to give the birds a song and the mountains a peak? Was he required to put stripes on the zebra and the hump on the camel? Would we have known the difference had he made the sunsets gray instead of orange? Why do stars have twinkles and the waves snowy crests? Why dash the cardinal in red and drape the beluga whale in white? Why wrap creation in such splendor? Why go to such trouble to give such gifts?

Why do *you?* You do the same. I've seen you searching for a gift. I've seen you stalking the malls and walking the aisles. I'm not talking about the obligatory gifts.

Hark!
The herald angels sing,
"Glory to the newborn King;
Peace on earth, and mercy mild;
God and sinners reconciled."

—CHARLES WESLEY, 1739

I'm not describing the last-minute purchase of drugstore perfume on the way to the birthday party. Forget blue-light specials and discount purchases; I'm talking about that extra-special person and that extra-special gift. I'm talking about stashing away a few dollars a month out of the grocery money to buy him some lizard-skin boots; staring at a thousand rings to find her the best diamond; staying up all night Christmas Eve, assembling the new bicycle. Why do you do it? You do it so the eyes will pop. You do it so the heart will stop. You do it so the jaw will drop. You do it to hear those words of disbelief, "You did this for *me?*"

That's why you do it. And that's why God did it. Next time a sunrise steals your breath or a meadow of flowers leaves you speechless, remain that way. Say nothing and listen as heaven whispers, "Do you like it? I did it just for you."

I'm about to tell you something you may find hard to believe. You're about to hear an opinion that may stretch your imagination. You don't have to agree with me, but I would like you to consider it with me. You don't have to buy it, but at least think about it. Here it is: *If you were the only person on earth, the earth would look exactly the same.* The Himalayas would still have their drama and the Caribbean would still have its charm. The sun would still nestle behind the Rockies in the evenings and spray light on the desert in the mornings.

If you were the sole pilgrim on this globe, God would not diminish its beauty one degree.

Because he did it all for you . . . and he's waiting for you to discover his gift. He's waiting for you to stumble into the den, rub the sleep from your eyes, and see the bright red bike he assembled, just for you. He's waiting for your eyes to pop and your heart to stop. He's waiting for the moment between the dropping of the jaw and the leap of the heart. For in that silence he leans forward and whispers: *I did it just for you.*

Find such love hard to believe? That's okay. Just because we can't imagine God's giving us sunsets, don't think God doesn't do it. God's thoughts are higher than ours. God's ways are greater than ours. And sometimes, out of his great wisdom, our Father in heaven gives us a piece of heaven just to show he cares.

THE GREAT HOUSE OF GOD

Majesty in the Midst of Mundane

The noise and the bustle began earlier than usual in the village. As night gave way to dawn, people were already on the streets. Vendors were positioning themselves on the corners of the most heavily traveled avenues. Store owners were unlocking the doors to their shops. Children were awakened by the excited barking of the street dogs and the complaints of donkeys pulling carts.

The owner of the inn had awakened earlier than most in the town. After all, the inn was full, all the beds taken. Every available mat or blanket had been put to use. Soon all the customers would be stirring and there would be a lot of work to do.

One's imagination is kindled thinking about the conversation of the innkeeper and his family at the breakfast table. Did anyone mention the arrival of the young couple the night before? Did anyone ask about their welfare? Did anyone comment on the pregnancy of the girl on the donkey? Perhaps. Perhaps someone raised the subject. But, at best, it was raised, not discussed. There was nothing *that* novel about them. They were, possibly, one of several families turned away that night.

Besides, who had time to talk about them when there was so much excitement in the air? Augustus did the economy of Bethlehem a favor when he decreed that a census should be taken. Who could remember when such commerce had hit the village?

No, it was doubtful that anyone mentioned the couple's arrival or wondered about the condition of the girl. They were too busy. The day was upon them. The day's bread had to be made. The morning's chores had to be done. There was too much to do to imagine that the impossible had occurred.

God had entered the world as a baby.

God Came Near

Once in royal David's city
Stood a lowly cattle shed,
Where a mother laid her Baby
In a manger for His bed.
Mary was that mother mild,
Jesus Christ her little child.

—Cecil Frances Alexander, 1848

Letting God Love You

*M*y daughters are too old for this now, but when they were young—crib-size and diaper-laden—I would come home, shout their names, and watch them run to me with extended arms and squealing voices. For the next few moments we would speak the language of love. We'd roll on the floor, gobble bellies, and tickle tummies and laugh and play.

We delighted in each other's presence. They made no requests to me, with the exception of "Let's play, Daddy." And I made no demands of them, except, "Don't hit Daddy with the hammer."

My kids let me love them.

But suppose my daughters had approached me as we often approach God. "Hey, Dad, glad you're home. Here is what I want. More toys. More candy. And can we go to Disneyland this summer?"

"Whoa," I would have wanted to say. "I'm not a waiter, and this isn't a restaurant. I'm your father, and this is our house. Why don't you just climb up on Daddy's lap and let me tell you how much I love you?"

Ever thought God might want to do the same with you? *Oh, he wouldn't say that to me.* He wouldn't? Then to whom was he speaking when he said, "I have loved you with an everlasting love" (JER. 31:3 NIV)? Was he playing games when he said, "Nothing . . . will ever be able to separate us from the love of God that is in Christ" (ROM. 8:39)? Buried in the seldom-quarried mines of the minor prophets is this jewel:

> The LORD your God is with you; the mighty One will save you.
>
> He will rejoice over you. You will rest in his love; he will sing
>
> and be joyful about you. (ZEPH. 3:17)

Note who is active and who is passive. Who is singing, and who is resting? Who is rejoicing over his loved one, and who is being rejoiced over?

We tend to think we are the singers and God is the "singee." Most certainly that is often the case. But apparently there are times when God wishes we would just be still and (what a stunning thought!) let him sing over us.

I can see you squirming. You say you aren't worthy of such affection? Neither

You are precious to him.
So precious that
he became like you so that
you would come to him.

was Judas, but Jesus washed his feet. Neither was Peter, but Jesus fixed him breakfast. Neither were the Emmaus-bound disciples, but Jesus took time to sit at their table.

Besides, who are we to determine if we are worthy? Our job is simply to be still long enough to let him have us and let him love us.

JUST LIKE JESUS

THE PROMISES OF THE MOMENT

What the Manger
Means to Me

God came as a baby,
giving and entrusting Himself to me.
He expects my personal life to be a "Bethlehem."
Am I allowing my natural life
to be slowly transformed
by the indwelling life of the Son of God?
God's ultimate purpose is
that His Son might be exhibited in me.

—OSWALD CHAMBERS

Looking for the Savior

Once there was a man whose life was one of misery. The days were cloudy, and the nights were long. Henry didn't want to be unhappy, but he was. With the passing of the years, his life had changed. His children were grown. The neighborhood was different. The city seemed harsher.

He was unhappy. He decided to ask his minister what was wrong.

"Am I unhappy for some sin I have committed?"

"Yes," the wise pastor replied. "You have sinned."

"And what might that sin be?"

"Ignorance," came the reply. "The sin of ignorance. One of your neighbors is the Messiah in disguise, and you have not seen him."

The old man left the office stunned. "The Messiah is one of my neighbors?" He began to think whom it might be.

Tom the butcher? No, he's too lazy. Mary, my cousin down the street? No, too much pride. Aaron the paperboy? No, too indulgent. The man was confounded. Every person he knew had defects. But one was the Messiah. He began to look for Him.

He began to notice things he hadn't seen. The grocer often carried the sacks to the cars of older ladies. *Maybe he is the Messiah.* The officer at the corner always had a smile for the kids. *Could it be?* And the young couple who'd moved next door. *How kind they are to their cat. Maybe one of them . . .*

With time he saw things in people he'd never seen. And with time his outlook on life began to change. The bounce returned to his step. His eyes took on a friendly sparkle. When others spoke he listened. After all, he might be listening to the Messiah. When anyone asked for help, he responded; after all this might be the Messiah needing assistance.

The change of attitude was so significant that someone asked him why he was so happy. "I don't know," he answered. "All I know is that things changed when I started looking for God."

Now, that's curious. The old man saw Jesus because he didn't know what he looked like. The people in Jesus' day missed him because they thought they did.

How are things looking in your neighborhood?

A GENTLE THUNDER

Somehow not only for Christmas
But all the long year through,
The joy that you give to others
Is the joy that comes back to you.
And the more you spend in blessing
The poor and lonely and sad,
The more of your heart's possessing
Returns to make you glad.

—JOHN GREENLEAF WHITTIER, 1866

A child has been born—for us!

The gift of a son—for us!…

His names will be: Amazing Counselor,

Strong God,

Eternal Father,

Prince of Wholeness.

—Isaiah 9:6 MSG

Come to the Party

A friend organized a Christmas cookie swap for our church office staff. The plan was simple. Price of admission was a tray of cookies. Your tray entitled you to pick cookies from the other trays. You could leave with as many cookies as you brought.

Sounds simple, if you know how to cook. But what if you can't? What if you can't tell a pan from a pot? What if, like me, you are culinary challenged? What if you're as comfortable in an apron as a body-builder in a tutu? If such is the case, you've got a problem.

Such was the case, and I had a problem. I had no cookies to bring; hence I would have no place at the party. I would be left out, turned away, shunned, eschewed, and dismissed. (Are you feeling sorry for me yet?)

This was my plight.

And, forgive me for bringing it up, but your plight's even worse.

God is planning a party . . . a party to end all parties. Not a cookie party, but a feast. Not giggles and chitchat in the conference room, but wide-eyed wonder in the throne room of God. . . .

There is only one hitch. The price of admission is somewhat steep. In order to come to the party, you need to be righteous. Not good. Not decent. Not a taxpayer or churchgoer.

Citizens of heaven are righteous. R-i-g-h-t.

All of us *occasionally* do what is right. A few *predominantly* do what is right. But do any of us *always* do what is right? According to Paul we don't. "There is none righteous, no, not one" (ROM. 3:10 NKJV). . . .

Who then is righteous? God is righteous. His decrees are righteous (ROM. 1:32). His judgment is righteous (ROM. 2:5). His requirements are righteous (ROM 8:4). His acts are righteous (DAN. 9:16). Daniel declared, "Our God is right in everything he does" (DAN. 9:14).

God is never wrong. He has never rendered a wrong decision, experienced the wrong attitude, taken the wrong path, said the wrong thing, or acted the wrong way. He is never too late or too early, too loud or too soft, too fast or too

With the loving mercy of our God,
a new day from heaven will dawn upon us.
It will shine on those who
live in darkness,
in the shadow of death.
It will guide us into the path of peace.

LUKE 1:78–79

slow. He has always been and always will be right. He is righteous.

When it comes to righteousness, God runs the table without so much as a bank shot. And when it comes to righteousness, we don't know which end of the cue stick to hold. Hence, our plight.

Will God, who is righteous, spend eternity with those who are not? If God accepted the unrighteous, the invitation would be even nicer, but would he be right? Would he be right to overlook our sins? Lower his standards? No. He wouldn't be right. And if God is anything, he is right.

He told Isaiah that righteousness would be his plumb line, the standard by which his house is measured (ISA. 28:17). If we are unrighteous, then, we are left in the hallway with no cookies. Or to use Paul's analogy, "we're sinners, every one of us, in the same sinking boat with everybody else" (ROM. 3:19 MSG). Then what are we to do?

Carry a load of guilt? Many do. So many do. And guilt can consume. . . .

So what do we do? Our Lord is right, and we are wrong. His party is for the guiltless, and we are anything but. What do we do?

I can tell you what I did. I confessed my need. Remember my Christmas cookie dilemma? This is the e-mail I sent to the whole staff. "I can't cook, so I can't be at the party."

Did any of the assistants have mercy on me? No.

Did any of the staff have mercy on me? No.

Did any of the Supreme Court justices have mercy upon me? No.

But a saintly sister in the church did have mercy on me. How she heard of my problem, I do not know. Perhaps my name found its way on an emergency prayer list. But I do know this. Only moments before the celebration, I was given a gift, a plate of cookies, twelve circles of kindness.

And by virtue of that gift, I was privileged a place at the party.

Did I go? You bet your cookies I did. Like a prince carrying the crown on a pillow, I carried my gift into the room, set it on the table, and stood tall. And because some good soul heard my plea, I was given a place at the table.

And because God hears your plea, you'll be given the same. Only, he did more—oh, so much more—than bake cookies for you.

It was, at once, history's most beautiful and most horrible moment. Jesus stood in the tribunal of heaven. Sweeping a hand over all creation, he pleaded, "Punish me for their mistakes. See the murderer? Give me his penalty. The adulteress? I'll take her shame. The bigot, the liar, the thief? Do to me what you would do to them. Treat me as you would a sinner."

And God did. "For Christ died for sins once for all, the righteous for the unrighteous, to bring you to God" (1 Pet. 3:18 niv).

Yes, righteousness is what God is, and, yes, righteousness is what we are not, and, yes, righteousness is what God requires. But "God has a way to make people right with him" (Rom. 3:21).

Not a cookies swap, but a guilt exchange. We give God our guilt in exchange for his grace.

One final thought about the Christmas cookie party. Did everyone know I didn't cook the cookies? If they didn't, I told them. I told them I was present by virtue of someone else's work. My only contribution was my own confession.

We'll be saying the same for eternity.

Traveling Light

Divine Gifts

Oh, the things we do to give gifts to those we love.

But we don't mind, do we? We would do it all again. Fact is, we *do* it all again. Every Christmas, every birthday, every so often we find ourselves in foreign territory. Grownups are in toy stores, Dads are in teen stores. Wives are in the hunting department, and husbands are in the purse department.

Not only do we enter unusual places, we do unusual things. We assemble bicycles at midnight. We hide the new tires with mag wheels under the stairs. One fellow I heard about rented a movie theater so he and his wife could see their wedding pictures on their anniversary.

And we'd do it all again. Having pressed the grapes of service, we drink life's sweetest wine—the wine of giving. We are at our best when we are giving. In fact, we are most like God when we are giving.

Have you ever wondered why God gives so much? We could exist on far less. He could have left the world flat and gray; we wouldn't have known the difference. But he didn't.

He splashed orange in the sunrise
and cast the sky blue.
And if you love to see geese as they gather,
chances are you'll see that too.

Did he have to make the squirrel's tail furry?
Was he obliged to make the birds sing?
And the funny way that chickens scurry
or the majesty of thunder when it rings?
Why give a flower fragrance? Why give food its taste?
Could it be
he loves to see
that look upon your face?

Thanks be to God
for his gift that is too wonderful
for words.

2 Corinthians 9:15

If we give gifts to show our love, how much more would he? If we—speckled with foibles and greed—love to give gifts, how much more does God, pure and perfect God, enjoy giving gifts to us? Jesus asked, "If you hardhearted, sinful men know how to give good gifts to your children, won't your Father in heaven even more certainly give good gifts to those who ask him for them?" (MATT. 7:11 TLB).

God's gifts shed light on God's heart, God's good and generous heart. Jesus' brother James tells us: "Every desirable and beneficial gift comes out of heaven. The gifts are rivers of light cascading down from the Father of Light" (JAMES 1:17 MSG). Every gift reveals God's love . . . but no gift reveals his love more than the gifts of the cross.

They came, not wrapped in paper, but in passion. Not placed around a tree, but a cross. And not covered with ribbons, but sprinkled with blood.

The gifts of the cross.

Much has been said about the gift of the cross itself, but what of the other gifts? What of the nails, the crown of thorns? The garments taken by the soldiers. The garments given for the burial. Have you taken time to open these gifts?

He didn't have to give them, you know. The only act, the only *required* act for our salvation was the shedding of blood, yet he did much more. So much more. Search the scene of the cross, and what do you find?

A wine-soaked sponge.

A sign.

Two crosses beside Christ.

Divine gifts intended to stir that moment, that split second when your face will brighten, your eyes will widen, and God will hear you whisper, "You did this for me?"

The diadem of pain
Which sliced your gentle face,
Three spikes piercing flesh and wood
To hold you in your place.

The need for blood I understand.
Your sacrifice I embrace.
But the bitter sponge, the cutting spear,
the spit upon your face?
Did it have to be a cross?

Did not a kinder death exist

than six hours hanging between life and death,

all spurred by a betrayer's kiss?

"Oh, Father," you pose,

heart-stilled at what could be,

"I'm sorry to ask, but I long to know,

did you do this for me?"

Dare we pray such a prayer? Dare we think such thoughts? Could it be that the hill of the cross is rich with God's gifts?

As you ponder what the manger means to you, unwrap God's gift of grace, the cross.

As you feel the timber of the cross and trace the braid of the crown and finger the point of the spike—pause and listen. Perchance you will hear him whisper:

"I did it just for you."

HE CHOSE THE NAILS

Seeking the Savior

Simeon [said], "Can I stay alive until I see him?"

The Magi [said], "Saddle up the camels. We aren't stopping until we find him."

The shepherds [said], "Let's go. . . . Let's see." . . .

They wanted the Savior. They wanted to see Jesus.

They were earnest in their search. One translation renders Hebrews 11:6: "God . . . rewards those who *earnestly* seek him" (NIV, italics mine).

Another reads, "God rewards those who *search* for him" (PHILLIPS, italics mine).

And another: "God . . . rewards those who *sincerely look* for him" (TLB, italics mine).

I like the King James translation: "He is a rewarder of them that *diligently* seek him" (italics mine).

Diligently—what a great word. Be diligent in your search. Be hungry in your quest, relentless in your pilgrimage. Let this book be but one of dozens you read about Jesus and this hour be but one of hundreds in which you seek him. Step away from the puny pursuits of possessions and positions, and seek your king.

Don't be satisfied with angels. Don't be content with stars in the sky. Seek him out as the shepherds did. Long for him as Simeon did. Worship him as the wise men did. . . . Risk whatever it takes to see Christ.

God rewards those who seek *him*. Not those who seek doctrine or religion or systems or creeds. Many settle for the lesser passions, but the reward goes to those who settle for nothing less than Jesus himself.

JUST LIKE JESUS

Away in a manger,

no crib for a bed,

the little Lord Jesus laid down

His sweet head.

The stars in the bright sky

looked down where He lay—

the little Lord Jesus,

asleep on the hay.

—MARTIN LUTHER, 1535

EPILOGUE

Silent Night of
the Heart

Yea, Lord, we greet Thee,

Born this happy morning;

O Jesus, to Thee be all glory given;

Word of the Father,

Now in flesh appearing:

O come, let us adore Him, . . .

Christ the Lord.

—TRANSLATED FROM LATIN BY F. OAKLEY, 1841

Do You See Him?

I t's Christmas night. The house is quiet. Even the crackle is gone from the fireplace. Warm coals issue a lighthouse glow in the darkened den. Stockings hang empty on the mantle. The tree stands naked in the corner. Christmas cards, tinsel, and memories remind Christmas night of Christmas Day.

It's Christmas night. What a day it has been! Spiced tea. Santa Claus. Cranberry sauce. "Thank you so very much." "You shouldn't have!" "Grandma is on the phone." Knee-deep in wrapping paper. "It just fits." Flashing cameras. . . .

It's Christmas night. The tree that only yesterday grew from soil made of gifts, again grows from the Christmas tree stand. Presents are new possessions. Wrapping paper is bagged and in the dumpster. The dishes are washed and leftover turkey awaits next week's sandwiches.

It's Christmas night. The last of the carolers appeared on the ten o'clock news.

God's help is near
and always available,
but it is only given to
those who seek it.

The last of the apple pie was eaten by my brother-in-law. And the last of the Christmas albums have been stored away having dutifully performed their annual rendition of chestnuts, white Christmases, and red-nose reindeers.

It's Christmas night.

The midnight hour chimed and I should be asleep, but I'm awake. I'm kept awake by one stunning thought. The world was different this week. It was temporarily transformed.

The magical dust of Christmas glittered on the cheeks of humanity ever so briefly, reminding us of what is worth having and what we were intended to be. We forgot our compulsion with winning, wooing, and warring. We put away our ladders and ledgers, we hung up our stopwatches and weapons. We stepped off our race tracks and roller coasters and looked outward toward the star of Bethlehem.

It's the season to be jolly because, more than at any other time, we think of him. More than in any other season, his name is on our lips.

And the result? For a few precious hours our heavenly yearnings intermesh and we become a chorus. A ragtag chorus of longshoremen, Boston lawyers, illegal immigrants, housewives, and a thousand other peculiar persons who are banking that Bethlehem's mystery is in reality, a reality. "Come and behold him" we sing, stirring even the sleepiest of shepherds and pointing them toward the Christ-child.

For a few precious hours, he is beheld. Christ the Lord. Those who pass the year without seeing him, suddenly see him. People who have been accustomed to using his name in vain, pause to use it in praise. Eyes, now free of the blindness of self, marvel at his majesty.

All of a sudden he's everywhere.

In the grin of the policeman as he drives the paddy wagon full of presents to the orphanage.

In the twinkle in the eyes of the Taiwanese waiter as he tells of his upcoming Christmas trip to see his children.

In the emotion of the father who is too thankful to finish the dinner table prayer.

He's in the tears of the mother as she welcomes home her son from overseas.

He's in the heart of the man who spent Christmas morning on skid row giving away cold baloney sandwiches and warm wishes.

And he's in the solemn silence of the crowd of shopping mall shoppers as the elementary school chorus sings "Away in the Manger."

Emmanuel. He is with us. God came near.

It's Christmas night. In a few hours the cleanup will begin—lights will come down, trees will be thrown out. Size 36 will be exchanged for size 40, eggnog will be on sale for half price. Soon life will be normal again. December's generosity will become January's payments and the magic will begin to fade.

But for the moment, the magic is still in the air. Maybe that's why I'm still awake. I want to savor the spirit just a bit more. I want to pray that those who beheld him today will look for him next August. And I can't help but linger on one fanciful thought: If he can do so much with such timid prayers lamely offered in December, how much more could he do if we thought of him every day?

God Came Near

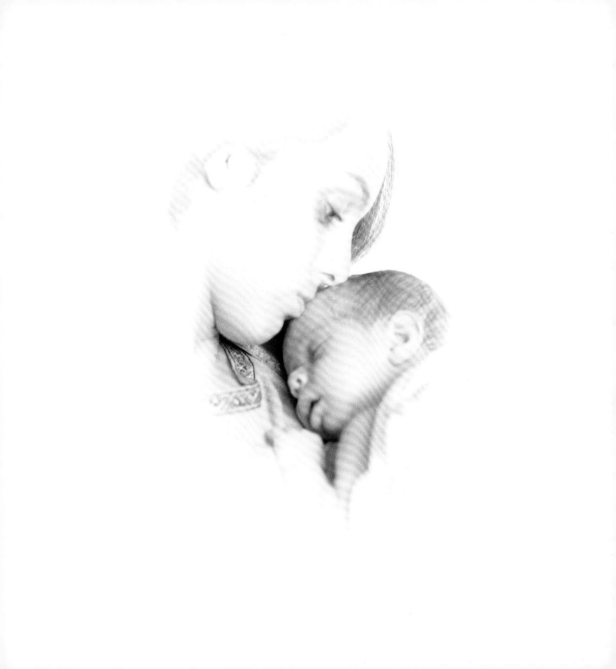

The gift
is not from man to God.
It is from God
to man.

Acknowledgments

Grateful acknowledgment is made to the following publishers for permission to reprint this copyrighted material. All copyrights are held by the author, Max Lucado.

The Applause of Heaven (NASHVILLE: W PUBLISHING GROUP, 1990).

In the Eye of the Storm (NASHVILLE: W PUBLISHING GROUP, 1991).

He Still Moves Stones (NASHVILLE: W PUBLISHING GROUP, 1993).

When God Whispers Your Name (NASHVILLE: W PUBLISHING GROUP, 1994).

A Gentle Thunder (NASHVILLE: W PUBLISHING GROUP, 1995).

In the Grip of Grace (NASHVILLE: W PUBLISHING GROUP, 1996).

Cosmic Christmas (NASHVILLE: W PUBLISHING GROUP, 1997).

The Great House of God (NASHVILLE: W PUBLISHING GROUP, 1997).

Just Like Jesus (NASHVILLE: W PUBLISHING GROUP, 1998).

When Christ Comes (NASHVILLE: W PUBLISHING GROUP, 1999).

God Came Near (SISTERS, ORE.: MULTNOMAH PUBLISHERS, 1987).

He Chose the Nails (NASHVILLE: W PUBLISHING GROUP, 2000).